April 17/2014.

On The Marches

Poems

by

Sir Michael Leighton, Bart.

Pictures

by

Mary Leighton- (née Parker)
and
Daughter, Frances Leighton

Edited by Michael Willmott

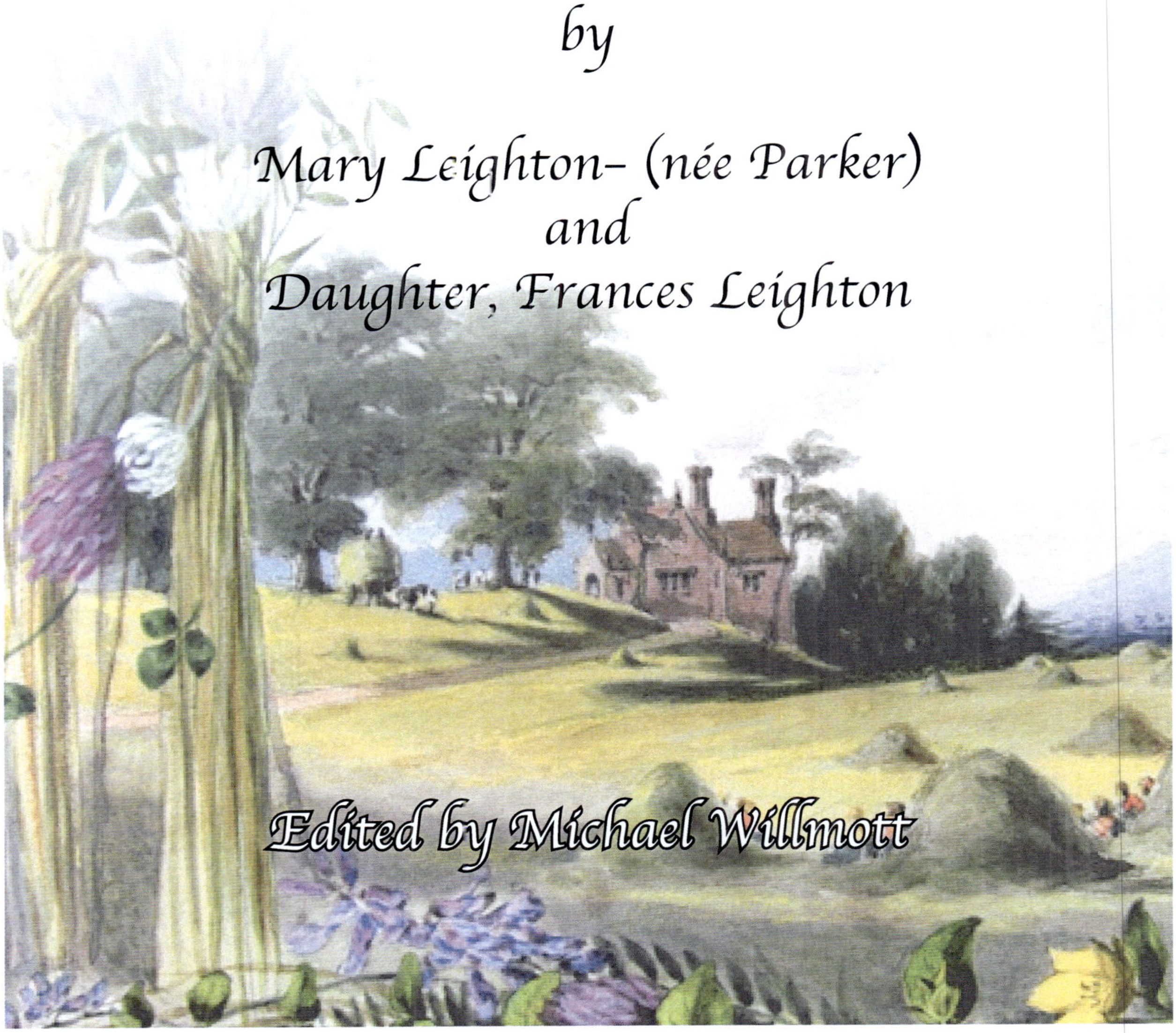

YouCaxton Publications
132 Frankwell, Shrewsbury, Shropshire. SY3 8JX
www.youCaxton.co.uk

Edited by Mike Willmott, Shrewsbury Words 01743 366933

Published in Great Britain by
Sir Michael Leighton

ISBN 978-0-9574414-0-8

Set in Adobe Garamond Pro

Printed and bound in Great Britain

Dedication

To all things beautiful

A Commendation

From an appreciation of an earlier collection of Sir Michael's poems, by *Dr Gladys Mary Coles*:

Sir Michael is a poet whose eloquence and lyricism link him at once with his ancestor Lord de Tabley (who just missed being selected as Poet Laureate). Sir Michael Leighton has much to say, his poetry is meaningful, and his vision far-seeing, based on a close, unshirking look at our world today. Perhaps the most significant poem in this (early) collection is The Dead Tribe, (see page - which begins,

There are no scavengers;
The sand has fled the hour-glass.
The warning was when the trees departed,
The rivers' sour corruption mantled this world.

This is a strong poem of warning from one who is a lover of nature, an ornitholcgist, a wildlife photographer, caring deeply about his own heritage and that of future generations. This poem ends on a hopeful note: 'Impatient perhaps, something stirs/ in the crust of the ashes, /eternal heritage'.

Sir Michael Leighton has his own distinctive voice, and is a born poet. Mary Webb, whose birthplace at Leighton was once part of the Leighton Estate owned by Sir Michael's ancestors, would certainly have appreciated his concern for nature, and feeling for its creatures.

A contribution from profits from the sale of this book will be made to

Hope House Children's Hospice, Morda, Oswestry

Editor's Introduction

In 1957, Sir Michael Leighton, Bart, inherited the extensive Loton Estate at Alberbury in Shropshire. It has its deer-park and its avenue, its lodges (English and Welsh) and its stables, its west end border with Wales, its fruitful Shropshire farmland, and the River Severn twining its way round its edges for three and a quarter miles.

When not attending to its upkeep and preservation, Sir Michael has a pastime which above all – even cooking – keeps his mind and soul alive: poetry. At his Norththaw Prep School he won a prize for his recitation of Sir Alfred Noyes' The Highwayman. (Characteristically, he can remember the mark – 49/50.) Then at Stowe, poetry was the subject for which he was given most praise. He now enjoys sharing poetry reading with his group of friends named after the local hill, Bryn-la-hope ('The cold hill on the top of the valley') in the Sunflower Theatre at Loton.

His great-uncle Lord de Tabley of Tabley House was tipped to be the mid-nineteenth century Poet Laureate, but was pipped at the post by Alfred, Lord Tennyson. Words and rhymes, and indeed some elements of the Victorian style, seem to reverberate in Sir Michael's mind in spontaneous, free associations: his poems appear in a gush of creativity.

It's been my job, and pleasure, and privilege, to work with Sir Michael, chiselling at the poems to organise them into an anthology. It has been a joy to have the luxury of finding appropriate art-work by his talented great-great-grandmother Mary Leighton,(née Parker) and her equally talented daughter Frances Leighton (who married the Rev Baldwin-Childe of Kerre Hall, Worcester). Both of these great Shropshire, Victorian artists, have hitherto received scant recognition, locally, or nationally. (A forthcoming book will remedy this situation.)

The title *'On the Marches'* emerged as fitting Sir Michael's love of his home and the surrounding locality, and because it is the place which has inspired his deepest thoughts and feelings.

Michael Willmott

Sir Michael Leighton

(as appeared in 'Country Life')

Foreword

The Leighton family crest is a mythical bird, the Wyvern. I feel sure Sir Michael would be equally happy with a Red Kite. Michael is very much a countryman at heart, with a deep love and respect for nature, and much of this passion is reflected in this anthology of poems.

Sir Michael Leighton's writing has shades of John Donne and Shakespeare, and he has certainly been influenced by the works of Matthew Arnold and W.H. Auden, which in itself is very thought-provoking.

It is through his writing and poetry that we discover the real Michael Leighton. There is a deep sensitivity of style, and a real understanding of things both seen and unseen. His early poems often had a brooding and dark melancholia, which could have been reflected in his own life at the time. Now, with wisdom of age, and an acceptance of his own mortality, his poetry is calm, with a spiritual quality which is often inspired by nature and the elements.

Howard Franklin,
President, Shrewsbury Decorative and Fine Arts Society

Heritage

We that are born with the silver spoon,
christened under the Harvest Moon,
our destiny locked in trust -
in-born heritage – don't let it rust.

Long graceful halls, cared for lovingly;
striking pictures draping the staircase walls.
History floats through every room -
memories from a forgotten age
quietly hold centre stage -
tell of Life's broken dreams -
romantic scenes.

Defiant souls still hold their sway -
they are from another day.
Outside at evening time
the garden warmth delights,
with poetry from byegone times –
children, nursery rhymes -
hopefully - for future times!

Sir Michael Leighton, 2012

Leighton Heraldry – Mary Parker

CONTENTS

DREAD SHAME

Church Walk, Loton Park– Mary Parker

The Spirits Of The Place

Home On The Marches

Home is
where the border runs,
through leafy lanes,
and meadows sweet.
Confluence where two rivers kiss,
then journey on their way,
the Severn carrying Vyrnwy to the sea:
they protect the border - it is their destiny.
Sleepy Welsh hillsides stand graceful on the Marches,
looking down on valleys, watchful – it's their task,
adorned by heavy, hanging woods,
mantling* the landscape,
like a vast dragon from fairy-tales.
Picturesque horizon -
endless carpets of green;
charismatic Border country –
peaceful, serene.

(to mantle = to spread wings for exercise, as a perched hawk does. OED)*

Alberbury Churchyard

Alberbury churchyard has a quietness of its own:
a labyrinth, time capsule — no one is alone.
The birdsong is different here:
it's dignified and strong.
Perhaps, in the singing, the spirits are the song.
Eternity, tranquillity —
are we really here that long?

High over Hafod

High over the hill, early morning,
before the sheep have stirred,
A soft, low, fluting call
drifts almost unheard.

Across the Hafod slopes and trees,
lifted by a cool, strong breeze,
effortless slow-motion flight
gladdens the heart - just the sight:
this is the valley of the kite!

A Red Kite

Rodney's Pillar

The Breidden Hills are washed in snow;
the Severn meanders down below -
the essence of the scenery.
For centuries now, amidst a descant of church chimes,
a silent Goddess has watched over her children on the forest floor,
and dreams on what has gone before:
Celts and Saxons strong,
who have walked these hills,
and now belong, to life eternal.
Serenely stands on crest of hill
Rodney's Pillar, ancient, still —
a silhouette of granite rock
built by man, as a silent clock:
a reminder of yet another long-gone war.

Breidden in the Distance - Mary Parker

Wild Edric's Watch

Across the Long Mynd, in the gloom,
before the shadows chase the moon,
the Devil in his chair sits,
hunched – grotesque – beware!

Here Wild Edric roams,
listening to the winds that moan,
a phantom of byegone times:
fables, stories, legends, rhymes,
the Stiperstones are his domain.

He hunts his hounds in wind and rain,
with Lady Godda by his side.
This is where they like to ride –
seldom seen, but often heard.

His baying hounds, his piercing cries
disturb the dead where they lie.
His mystic, eery blowing calls
alert the mist-filled morn.

Legend says he has the right
to scatter spirits of the night,
but in the day it is his task
to guard our country's threatened shores.

Wild Edric listens on his hill
for voices bearing tidings ill:
if they are heard from across the sea,
there is danger for our destiny.

Sir Michael as Wild Edric on 'Sloopy' at Oakley Park, 1976

A.E. Housman - Requiescat

The Shropshire hills are silent -
mystic - shrouded still.
Shadows in the twilight play,
in their merry, short-lived way.

Longmynd, Lawley, Caradoc,
hosts to bygone tales,
Stiperstones, Devil's Chair -
where wild Edric roams,
hunting his hounds
with bleeding, tingling tones.
(Beware - the country groans.)

Then there is Clee Hill:
your mind still wanders there.
Pontesford, Nescliffe, Wrekin, Grinshill,
proudly stand, a rich vein, and tall -
our heritage, our land.

For you, A. E. Housman, their beauty lingers still:
your verses pause amongst them,
as does your pen and quill.
Shropshire Hills - a memory, a monument
set fair - have honoured your commitments,
and answered with a prayer.

Peacocks in Paradise

In a quiet Welsh valley
once stood a proud mansion:
statuesque, hanging trees, garden slopes
to the Ystwyth at her knees:
a poignant time poised with grace,
vanished without trace.
Monuments of broken stone, cold figures:
they are guardians from the past.
The valley mourns —
but memories last,
of peacocks in paradise.

Hafod Mansion - John Warwick Smith (1810)

Ladies of Llangollen

From Ireland, the Emerald Isle,
two ladies fled across the sea,
Llangollen-bound,
left their country's social whirl
to begin a life anew.
Their friendship strong would see them through,
beyond the havoc they had strewn.

Plas Newyth gave a quiet, contented life,
where they entertained folk from all walks of life,
Royalty, locals, family, saw them as their friends.
The ladies made a garden in the vale,
a life's work of beauty in repose,
from pergola to tall trees,
statues, rock plants, and wild rose.

The ladies' fame spread far and wide,
brought many celebrities by carriage-ride
to hear the tales that they would tell
of former sadness — cold grand halls
for which they did not care.
Plas Newyth replaced their emerald home,
in Wales deep in the vale.

Deep respect was paid by all who crossed their paths:
in market-place, stately homes throughout the land,
they were welcomed, hand in hand.
Their legend will never die –
why two fine ladies chose to fly
from their natural home,
to be at peace,
and — together — live alone.

Ladies of Llangollen - Mary Parker

Santes Melangell

(Plethyn Byer a Bod)

She graces the hillside's purple light —
a silhouette in simple white —
stark contrast to the dark wet night.
Her sensuous form in the morning air
bewitches the breeze through long flowing hair
as she bends to shield from baying hounds
the frightened bundle in her arms.
Sanctuary bound —
for in the chapel there's a shrine
that tells how a long, long time ago
an Irish lass was moved to save the hunted hare.
Protect forever creatures there
that play above the bryn.

Pennant Melangell – Mary Parker

Summer's Day - The Dovey

The tall pines high on the ridge;
the train triumphant across the bridge;
cattle, languid pastures graze;
the village church drones songs of praise;
the river, a jewel silver line
simmering, gossamer fine;
soft-coloured banks of flowers,
touched by bees, who search for hours
to build their honey domes.

Curlew pipe their fluting calls;
sand-pipers bobbing shingle-bound.
The joy of spring — nature's sound —
spoilt, as homeward bound
rubber-booted chariots race:
another day, another face.

Cwmystwyth

For Audrey

The Welsh hills beckon,
brooding over mystic times.
Mists surrender to their beauty.

The silent mines yearn to tell of bygone struggles,
while the Ystwyth, true to her name,
winds, turns and tumbles, laughing, to the sea,
as the ghosts of Pendry keep watch for eternity,
and high, high over Hafod, my heart, my soul.

Driftwood

The driftwood waltzes with the tide:
seabirds, sentinels ride, swaying to the water's strength.

Standing out, white sails, anchored boats,
dressed seaweed swamps, rotting posts,
have once been trees,
now at the mercy of buffeting seas –
then decay in repose.

Frayed ropes, green-stained chains
sculpted by sand, sea and rains;
just the roar from the mighty sea:
in confinement, withered tree.

Criccieth – Seaside

White horses distant run;
the call of gulls, weakening sun;
boats in the harbour pull at their chains,
riding on the tide,
buffeting the wharf.

Storms have washed litter from promenade
to pier – (not of the realm) –
but left empty bottles parted from their beer,
while lobster-pots are bobbing gracefully,
out at sea.

Home-made bread, and milk-shake bars bring memories
back to me.

Criccieth – Judy Leighton

River Severn Flood

I am surplus - over the riverbank -
I invade ditches, meadows feed:
I have become an inland sea.

Creatures from the earth flee:
devastation follows me.
My outstretched arms caress the ground:
I'm here awhile, but make no sound.

But in the stillness, something stirs:
Sabrina, river goddess, will command,
as ever-watchful she will be,
her message clear and plain:
'Get thee hence, to the open sea!'

Harlech Castle – Frances Leighton

The Welsh Bridge, Shrewsbury

I've stood alone for many years -
silent, sombre, remote.
My weathered stones are like old bones,
but my feet are secured in mud.

I stand fast against the flow,
guarding where the waters go,
sometimes high, sometimes low,
busy in the winter rains,
cuffing against my worn down chin.

Quiet in the summer time,
a refuge for bobbing sticks and things,
I watch the fishermen in the early hours
sprawl beneath my gaze,
crouched on man-made seats,
smoke, and eat their fill,
attempting to catch the fish at play.

Many folk saunter over my arches,
while under me ride coloured boats and canoes;
fast, silent, racing crews
stretch their limbs in eights and fours and twos.

So my life is never dull, as I hold a watching brief
of creatures that pass beneath:
sandmartins flirting at the flies,
cormorants vying for fishermen's catch,
seagulls protesting, an inland choir.

I then at twilight watch the otters play -
and reflect upon my crowded day,
alone no more.

The Severn

The source of the Hafren,
my birthplace, my home,
has sent me on my journey,
has commanded me to roam
through the valley, across the hills.
I idle past the woollen mills
through market towns penned with sheep.
They graze my banks on either side.
They've been my friends for my long, long ride,
for I am the longest British river,
bound to pay homage to the sea:
Vyrnwy and Banwy, they will follow me.
They are my son, my daughter,
my watery family tree.
The Border County looms ahead —
I begin to slow.
This is where I stretch myself,
this is where I need a tow.
Here Mother Nature takes a hand
as I spill myself upon the land,
flooding the farmers' fields afar
breaking my shoulders,
filling the streams,
and then the dykes,
creating ponds and lakes
the likes that are not seen before,
settling myself, and through the shires
I bend and slide for hours and hours.
Bristol is my destiny:
I've covered very many miles.
I do this for eternity.

The Severn at Shrawardine - Mary Parker

Cedars Of Lebanon

Graceful cedars dip and sway,
their thoughts are from another day:
great parks, baronial halls,
cricket grounds — quiet applause,
carriages, exotic cars,
sweet beneath are strong, tall towers;
children play below our feet,
white-clothed lunches laid — a treat!
We've seen changes come and go,
lost limbs to heavy snow,
played host to birds and bees,
felt drought, lack of rain,
morning, day, night the same.
We will stand the test of time,
children's laughter, nursery rhyme.
Sun shows our profile kissed
and evening shadows in the mist.

Loton Cedars

The Spirit of Great Britain

Lament: Great Britain

The pearls have fled the oyster-beds:
politicians, severed heads,
chivalry almost dead.
Will we hear the lion roar?
Will the 'few' still protect our shore?
Will stately homes be no more?
Will we hear our heritage's protesting tones?
Britannia in her chariot roams.

Stonehenge

Their mystery stands in shadow, then exposed:
a parliament of broken rock has stood the time;
hunched shoulders grace their grassy shrine,
as in the mists of time, the stones stand still.

Are their secrets never heard —
wandering sheep, quiet fox, croaking bird?
Then a screaming aeroplane passes overhead again.
Solitude will cause a smile
for they have been here, ancient pile —
memories — no broken bones;
an earthy elegance:
strong, proud stones.

Burial of Arthur

Sunlight:
early mist -
the falcon flown from the wrist.
Two lovers in a tryst
steal away before they're missed,
laughing at a stolen kiss,
while back in the castle, all is gloom,
as knights, courtiers, horse and groom
bow their heads at Arthur's burial barge,
drifting to his graveyard out at sea.
as high on the hill,
on bended knee
the piper plays a last lament.

The Fallen – The Boer War

Battle of Ladysmith, Northern Natal, 1899

The merciless, hollow call of the drum;
the acrid smell of the smoking gun;
the sapper lies in the tortuous sun;
across the desert just the hum of flies,
and shades of vultures dropping from the sky,
to clear dead horses from the scene,
just white bones shining clean.

The fallen have an open grave,
no monument to tell their tale,
the heroic braves are homeless now.
For them, scavengers in the distance howl.

Royal Flying Corps

(56 Squadron 1914-18 War)

High up in the empty blue
the brave, caring, charismatic few -
aristocrats of the air,
difficult to compare -
throw their planes across the sky,
the enemy to deny.
Their memory holds a special place,
for they are orphans in space.

D-Day

Swaying flowers of Northern France;
gently wave the vineyards;
tall avenues of poplars strong
join the peasant throng,
as on their bicycles they go.

But memories tell another tale
of how this place was blitzed to hell,
débris scattered everywhere —
chaos beyond repair;
how it was saved by brave, brave men,
so France could lift her head again,
by men from just across the sea —
courageous, full of dignity.

Never, France, forget your allies
in the battles fought
to save another nation's pride:
we rallied, on the morning tide.

Cease Fire

8TH MAY, 1945

It came on the wind, then the rain,
the silence - no more pain -
so that we will live our lives at last:
no fear from the Germans blast
nor rattling guns in early morn
would leave our bodies, souls, bleeding, torn,
by heavy bombs thrown down at dusk.
Warning, the banshee wail has made old folk
and children pale.
But all of this has ceased to be.
So kneel and pray on bended knee
that we will watch the poppies grow,
and hear the drone of the honeybee.

The White Cliffs Of Dover

Serenely stand the cliffs.
Below - sweeping sands, tranquil sea.
Children play on bended knee:
no brutality, no fuss,
just the rumbling village bus
trundling quietly to and fro.

But that was just a year ago,
before the war that brought us shame:
too much suffering, pain,
emotion, loss of name.

The great wall of Kent remains,
fortress defiant: pure-white flame!

Ode To Winston Churchill

He has led us through darkness, back into light,
from the cold grey dawn, and the black of the night.
He has taught us courage, and the will to fight;
to have faith in ourselves, our country, and King:
that we were the bee, but he was the sting;
to sacrifice life, for the good of mankind;
to stay out in front, and not fall behind.

Now is his glory for ever well read:
his great soul to heaven, the angels have fed.
Now England must make her own way - if she can –
and honour this noble, and gifted man,
who has given us peace, and saved us from shame.
He has gone from our lives, for ever more;
gone from his England: this Great Man o' War.

The Lone Soldier

He stands alone on crest of hill,
a single soldier, silent, still.
He represents the times before –
of those thousands killed in war.

Beneath is written bold in stone
Words that forever stand alone:
LET US NOW PRAISE GALLANT MEN -
THE LIKE WE MAY NOT SEE AGAIN.

The years have passed now – ten decades:
memories, hopefully, will not fade
of all those who marched away,
never to return this way.

The lone soldier, high on the hill -
a constant reminder of sad times,
as skipping lambs beneath him play,
welcoming another day.

The Last Tommy

for Harry Patch (1898-2009)

So he's gone to rest his head, at last -
our brave warrior from the past -
gone to join the friends he knew,
who fought with him – 'the famous few'.

Their battle-cry is heard no more,
for he himself has closed the door.
Let the world not forget -
for as time passes memories dim
of what we really thought of him,
and his valiant comrades too.

They sacrificed the life they knew:
there is no praise too great for them.
There is nothing left, but we have their names.
They stood so still, fair and tall,
waiting for the bugle-call.

The Cenotaph

In Alberbury Village stands before the crest of hill
a Cenotaph, elegant, proud, beautiful, and still,
for it bears the names of brave men,
who fought to save us all.

Through their courage, with backs against the wall,
their tomorrows, loves, sorrows,
in one flashing moment went.
Let us who are left, never forget their lives spent:
wrecked ships, burnt planes, tattered tents.

How best can we repay these souls?
Just watch the poppies fall,
our legacy to all of them:
keep on walking tall!

The War Memorial, Alberbury

© Andy Neal

The Spirit of Nature

Dawn

There comes a stillness,
just before the wakening shadows steal away.
The lilting breeze lifts and sighs,
heralding the day.

Leaves, under hedgerows, tossed there by the wind -
the morning rush – blackbirds scold –
the trotting fox, with swinging brush,
crosses the meadows – hears the curlew's fluting call.

The motionless heron, reed-like, standing tall.
Then the heavy bang from the old barn door –
'Morning has broken.'

Silver Fish

for Dig

Silver fish, on journey north
to the wide, open sea,
from ancestral river runs,
never trouble-free.
He has the gauntlet fought -
sometimes stayed awhile.

His graceful form in midstream
always causes a smile –
perhaps a missed heartbeat,
as we watch the water boil:
quivering silver symbol,
beautiful to see,
slips quietly to the ocean,
rejoicing to be free:

Salamander Pisces!

Pisces

The light of alertness springs and ends
in pounding waves of passion.
Upon the shore, hanging cliffs bow their heads,
staring far into the surf, guarding secrets.

A protesting strength of mystic times,
over the bar horizon bound;
perennial seas caress the sand,
keeping memories secure,
locked in dark abyss.

And in Pandora's box perhaps,
a written word of love survives,
crusted in jewels of green,
while sentinels kneeling at Neptune's throne,
endure eternity.

The Month of June - Mary Parker

Ode to the Mountain Lion

The mountain lion's mating call
disturbs the packhorse in its stall,
alerts all creatures, forest bound
that hear his commanding, eerie sound
rebound through mountain forests' heavy mists,
The spotted prince, on danger's list,
he has no fears, nor has he peers,
in the realm he owns -
walks alone, no family ties:
a species on the edge of life will survive
if all forest firs and pine are left in peace
until the end of time.

Savannah

I feel the magic of this land
never far away from me.
The valley lies below my feet,
the sparkle where two rivers meet.
Gently swaying savannah grass
caresses the wild geese as they pass.
Herds of bison tread this ground.
Are they shadows from the past,
like their proud hunting warrior tribes
who on this vastness used to ride?

The savannah has its beauty still —
unspoilt plains — giant hill.
Strong winds will forever blow:
keep the forest free from snow.
The eerie sound of the hunting wolf
scares wild horses to the hoof.
Overhead an eagle cries,
majestic, floating through the skies.
High on crest of hill
the lone feathered arrow quivers still.

Birds' Return

Graceful across the sky -
pilgrimage of the unknown -
many thousand miles have flown
their destiny a temporary home.
They have ridden storms, across the seas,
deserts, mountain canopy:
an inborn desire to reproduce -
the future flower of youth.
They decorate the skies, seas and shores,
trees, buildings - no applause -
just a joy to behold:
Nature's gift, to young and old.

Storm

Folding clouds, purple hue,
a labyrinth of cotton wool
passes slowly overhead,
cascading watershed
does not blow or overflow,
anoints the earth, a cleansing blow,
a helping hand for things that grow,
open fields, tall hedge-row,
keeps the river clear, sweet,
and tests the heron's treading feet,
then descends in crashing, frightening tones,
spring-cleans the ground and all that dwells
in garden, woodland,
down the dell,
then will slowly drift away,
as one lone blackbird in the quietness sings —
holds his sway.

The Falcon

As fast as Concorde,
but silent as the grave:
the destruction of lesser foes
at the tilt of one wing.
A bloody dust of feathers
marks her hunting presence,
and the smoking chimneys on the skyline
are ignorant, in their own bliss.

Rookery

They chatter, clatter in penthouse trees -
a parliament holding sway.
'The farmer's friend', (so they say -
but they frighten them away.)
Clad in blue-black dress,
their spring chorus soothes our stress:
to hear them gang at evening time -
part of nature's natural rhyme,
as in one large black cloud they fly,
anxious not to make a pie.

The Hunt

We sprang him in Butcher's Rush -
a handsome chap, with trailing brush.
We trailed his scent for mile on mile:
this really was a fox with style.
Over the railway bank with style,
we're flagging now, in single file
driven in the vale, we hunt him still.
Our bell-like tones have much to tell,
as all in one we cross the fell,
and 'feather' on the crest.
We've lost him as we cross the peat:
The clever fellow's doused his feet:
a simple trick, but rather neat.
But on the wind we hear the call:
the huntsman's blowing home for all,
to rest our aching bones.
While horsemen to their warm snug homes,
so Charlie in his earth will rest,
and lift his leg – a parting jest.

Month of October - Mary Parker

The Dead Tribe

There - are no scavengers;
the sand has fled the hour-glass.
The warning was when the trees departed:
the rivers' sour corruption mantled the world.
Biblical words became reality,
and the chiefs stumbled
over the bodies of their dead Indians.
Judge not mankind,
for it is their wont:
the spoils, like some emptying volcano,
tumble through photographic images,
the ages forever a Roman tableau,
and the void stands out - a shadow burnt:
remains - the Crucifixion.
Whispering sands - strong voices - the sea -
stubborn, loyal, searching: they were natural allies.
Beauty destroyed the cry, where no hill stood.
Underneath all a mighty curiosity lies
in abeyance, or repose.
The planets puzzled: no intrusion -
Mankind likened to the Dodo.
All is not dust:
Earth can grow again, and Life.
Impatient perhaps, something stirs,
in the crust of the ashes -
eternal heritage -
for the Gods are angry.

Songs of the Seasons

The song of summer stirs the day:
children run, tumble, play
round the maypole at the fair —
joyful laughter everywhere.

Autumn plays a different tune:
descant 'neath the harvest moon
echoes through the tops of trees,
dances with fallen leaves —
choir singing.

Winter song, festive time:
carols sung, chanting rhyme;
lanterns lead down the path
to old folks nestling by their hearths.

In the changing time of spring
a melody of fluting sounds dwell in hedgerows,
woods, rivers, fields.
As the crops promise yields
the skylark high in the air
sends a message for all to hear:
Happiness will conquer Fear!

Yesterday

Across the lonely purple hill
the march of time has stood so still,
stained the rocks, mountainsides.
Watch the kites, buzzards glide
while hosts of sheep down the dell
listen to the farmer's yell.

Broken roads, protesting carts –
the rasp of hooves as they try to pass -
that was many years ago.
Heavy mist, driven snow -
memories of Postman Joe -
different times, forgotten laughter;
nursery rhymes:
the apple peel, orange rind
left by the path near the rotting sign.
Once it went somewhere out of sight,
now keeps secrets: they have the right.

Apocalyptic Visions

Warning I

If the wind should cease to be
a burning echo, shadows flee
images from bygone years:
broken arrows, axes, spears,
confusion, tears.
Is there a movement down on earth,
as large white boulders crash?
Will they still a future find?
Architect - the earth's wide womb;
Reality - a giant tomb.
Yet there is life, as quietness reigns.
Now the echo fades:
Life will stir in rich vastness,
the 'Everglades':
the honeybees, alert, may never sting,
as mushrooms now are dancing round their ring.

Warning 2

If the global warming comes -
burns natural food supplies,
dries up watersheds -
nothing grows, there is no rain -
just empty beds of hollow ground.
Creatures there won't make a sound.
The human race, its time has come:
Cupid will not string his bow —
his darts have nowhere else to go.
Will it ever really snow?

Swaddling Clothes

An image blown across the sky
paints my thoughts and reasons why we exist.
Creation will not pass us by.
Reproduce – multiply –
hear the new-born cry.
Rejoice - lift up your heart -
and tread not on the scarecrow's tattered scarf.

Rape

Robbers of eternal youth,
decaying trees, gruesome truth,
tall hedgerows bleed
like severed limbs;
wild flowers shrink in despair;
pollution battles with fresh air.
Butterflies in circles strong
once graced woodland glades,
where overhead skylarks sang
in wild fields untilled by man.
But now we have a different tune:
a rasping, tedious sound
disturbs the quietness of the day,
and won't be told to go away.
I pray the silent evening come.

Winter Morning

Darkness surrenders to the dawn:
hedgerows' artistic frozen form;
grasses whispering tales to tell,
as the wind turns to hail.
Steamy cattle graze near walls.
The sea thunders its applause,
as grey geese far out at sea
are talking, searching company,
lifting from the tide in one great wave,
their hunger to appease.

Alert wild ponies in the bay -
their coats crusted, frosty grey.
Gulls cluster, bargains find -
ride the water's ebbing flow.
Wrecked ships crunch against the rocks:
they have nowhere else to go.

Three Score Years And Ten

I will make my way to the water's edge:
no seas, no trees, no sky,
no tomorrow, no reason why —
only yesterday, and many passers-by.
The local life tires,
while the piper on the hill
hauntingly intones reality.
Time is standing still.
The jester in his coloured coat
has written with his quill.

The Singer, Not The Song

It is the singer, not the song;
it is the striker, not the gong;
the preacher teaches right from wrong;
the orator holds the throng;
the general, when wars go wrong:
perhaps the singer's sung his song?

Eleanor (2008)

Your laughter, smile
lifts the day;
no adornment to hold your sway:
gazelle-like on the playing fields -
a natural on the stage,
and in the classroom too.
I am happy God made me
to be a part of you:
young, graceful branch from an ancient tree:
come down the path of life,
and follow me.

Eleanor Leighton, 2008

The Tramp

I tread up winter's muddy path
my natural bed to find,
a host of crows for company,
but soon are left behind.

I lay my head in an old sheeps' barn —
they scatter, then are gone.
Tomorrow will be market day:
folk are generous, work and play -
they know my needs.

I feel at ease
in jostling crowds:
my lonely life it feeds.
I chose to live life this way —
no real hassle, fuss -
no irritating people on an overcrowded bus —
just the joy of nature's way:
for all her gifts are free.

The large, tall trees like temples stand —
I feel they beckon me.
I catch a whisper in their swaying tops —
a message carried on the wind,
plain - audible to hear.
It lingers in the morning air:
'You're an eccentric millionaire!'

Oscar

(Mr Wilde's Play – *'The Importance of being Earnest'*)

They may have dimmed what lights they have,
and settled down on crude small wooden chairs.
On stage young Algy strolls with arrogant ease,
while Jimmie steals himself, and tries to please.

Enter Jack Worthing, jovial, sometimes demure:
he plays his part in earnest.
But tremble not as Lady Bracknell comes:
a tyrant no, but uppercrust — elegant without the bust.

Young Gwendolen and tall Cecily play the game of love,
on guard against each other,
confused by someone's brother:
they both stand fast until the last,
confronting one another.

But how, now, Dr. Chasuble in heavy disguise,
for he plays to poor Miss Prism before her very eyes.
And if you watch and listen to Mr Wilde's play,
note, in earnest, the important fact of the day:

crucial evidence –
a handbag -
in a railway station,
down Victoria way.

Over Milk Wood

Warm lights from the cottages in the village;
contented sheep are feeding:
Vicar Jones has missed his bus again.
Worse – for it pours with rain,
and at the side of the road
a little dead bird lies bleeding.

'Tis morning now — the folk awake.
Mrs. Humphreys bakes her cake.
The boys from school play near the stream
with their laughter, shouts of freedom:
they have no doubt Vicar Jones has his bicycle today.
But he is sneezing,
and at the side of the road
the little dead bird is cold.

Wedding today — what an event!
All is so much colour,
and in the garden a huge tent
with people from far and mostly near,
swilling down the local beer,
and chatting away the hours
amongst so many bowls of flowers,
and plates of food, and still more beer!
Red-faced Vicar Jones gives his "Blessing":
quiet in the evening time.
The church clock speaks, but cannot rhyme,
and the little dead bird,
by the side of the road, is gone.

Pipes of Pan

Listen to the pipes of Pan:
their haunting, fluting, tones
echo from the mountain tops,
cascading falling stones.

They tell of how the world began,
flowers, trees, all things tall,
creatures large, creatures small,
massive avi-fauna, awesome wing and claw.
Ground-trembling reptiles disrupt the forest floor,
proclaiming how the universe is swept with rain,
raging storms uplift the trees,
tumbling rocks have broken knees.

Then all is calmness: mystic seas
have strewn their seeds in disarray;
the pipes lie broken, cannot play -
small, wafer-like, thin, decay.

But on the hill, in the mists of time,
a ray of burning light, a shrine?
Is there someone standing there?
Flowing cloak, golden hair?
or is there really no one there?

Déjà vu

I feel I walked across the sea —
no ships nor boats to bother me —
just horizon, pale green:
a never-ending awesome scene.

An inner light will guide me,
For then there's land — the golden shore.
I feel I've been this way before,
just pure whites

No footprints, no strong hand:
a message washed away by an angry sand
perhaps was here for me to see:
did it read my destiny?

How did I walk across the sea?
I kneel, and pray - for company.

The Holocaust

Jupiter collides with Mars:
Time is obliterated.
Debris scatters stars
like canopies of frozen flowers.

Contrasting glares,
smouldering ore,
cascading galaxies galore,
tear at the earth's protesting floor.

Ruptured landscapes,
tidal waves,
Uplifted headstones
tossed from graves.

Time will settle –
fire, water, dust:
Memories –
not allowed to rust.

So what survives this holocaust,
in the gloom?
A sudden shaft of piercing brightness
spotlights the awesome sight.

A messenger, clad in white:
the burning pile of rubble is his throne.
And in His hand,
the Book of Wrong and Right.

The Grave Of My Friend

The old man was right — the world was sad.
The sun was strong: it was the month of May,
in this place to be buried in, in the shadow of the hills,
where animals of night do jest,
and the hawk makes his kills.

"I envy him," I said aloud, although he's left his home.
"Envy the dead," the old man had said,
"It is the dead that are alone."

Then he was gone across the field,
his spade and cap in hand,
left me alone in my sadness to sprinkle a little sand.
"Speak to me from the cold earth,
tell me you're glad that I came."

But the wind was silent, and answered with rain.
The old man was right, his words ring in my ears,
but I do not see, nor can I hear,
for in my eyes are tears.

Ride On!

Ride on – do not linger here:
Emotion, stress will appear.
Clinging to the forest's dripping trees
hangs a sweet, but cold rain.
My horse strides out across the ride.
I feel his strength, admire his stride.
Ride on – go from here,
As morning mists begin to clear.
I touch his flanks – swift he went –
seemed to know which road!
Carried me to pastures new,
seldom trodden by the few.
Ride on, I hear again,
my gallant steed,
his pace now slow.
Does he know which way to go?
The sun has set:
the afterglow –
radiant light –
casts shadows in the night.
My steed now has a gentle gait,
perhaps suspicious of our fate.
Have we reached the Golden Gate?
Is it closed? Are we too late?
There is a fine large apple tree,
close to the heavenly gate.
I see a gentle man – Adam -
on bended knee.
He observes a serpent underneath
with an apple gorged
beween its teeth – lifeless.
(Eve looks on, in disbelief.)

Old Year, New Year

"My run is over, once was new:
I hand my troubles, times, and gifts to you.
They will not cease, and will bewilder you –
The fallen snow, the Christmas tree,
flooded plains, teeming rain,
then even stronger gales again.

The heat of summer sun
all too short its course ran.
Bustling crowds everywhere –
rich folk dancing, worse for wear.
poor children in tattered clothes
embarrassed, hide themselves:
they feel unease, sometimes despair.
They've problems – no-one cares.

The gifts I pass to you –
something borrowed, something new –
Beauty, Sadness – just a few."

Then all will start again –
another reign will host the past,
and face the new, in the morning
test what's true.

Darwin's 'Theory'

Is this the way the world began:
mountains, seas, giant trees,
acres of golden sands, multitudes of rivers running wild,
prehistoric, rambling vegetation;
floral rainbow splashes, colour beams in wild profusion?
The world sprang from ashes;
firelight eclipsed the sun:
planet Earth was born.
No memory, no reason, no rhyme.
Was this Earth's true axis, or was it pitched off course?
Darwin gave us his solution to the mystery of Man -
the links between the creatures
grotesque, gigantic, divine,
which inhabited the earth -
our forefathers perhaps,
before the Virgin birth?

Easter

If I could walk, or talk, with Thee –
of the riddle of the apple-tree -
of the fishes, loaves of bread –
of Moses, puzzled by what You said –
the sea divided – road to Galilee -
with You – who told the cripple, 'Walk away' -
the Ten Commandments – how to live -
testing our frailty -
please, in Your prayers,
shed a tear,
for all lost souls:
You - the sacrifice for all our sins -
too much to understand.
But in the morning's quiet - soft light –
the stone from the tomb –
a sight to behold –
has rolled away.

Timeless Spirits

Stone In The Wood

Roughly hewn from granite rock,
faceless, unsculptured —
do not mock —
stands alone in woodland glade,
unmoved in sunlight, darkness, shade,
silhouette against the sky;
has heard wolves, badgers, foxes cry,
felt the wind, driving rain,
Summer's softness,
pain,
solitude:
will remain.

The Lantern

Hanging in the tree,
is it there for warmth — company?
Is it there to show the way —
a milestone for those that stray from the path they wish to tread?

The lantern cannot shake its head, or speak its mind —
Only the flickering of its flame
with its rustic prison swinging to and fro,
guards the blackness of the night.

Thoughts

Will the wilderness claim to be sanctuary
for those that flee?
Perhaps deny their destiny?

The Tree of Life its leaves will tell —
secrets from the wishing-well.

Hark the tolling of the bell,
ringing for all to hear,
as if the world has shed a tear,
for those that take each other's life —
or lose it by the surgeon's knife.

Floods that have no Noah's Ark:
is this the reality the prophets said would be,
the universe destroyed by man?
The rust crumbles on the watering-can.

Volcanic Inferno

The furnace in the mountain glows,
restless, glowering in repose,
tumbling coals threaten,
release their tension on the world,
spilling embers that unroll,
scorch and scour the protesting earth,
blankets of ashes remain.

The eruption passes — leaves the pain.
Sulphur plumes drift away,
then in their wake, decay,
burning Rembrandts of yesterday.

Eclipse

If this should be exposure of what is right,
it reveals a tortured mind – ecstacy -
something beyond our sight -
atmosphere with hidden bliss —
perhaps an angel's kiss -
the edge of life — a dark abyss?

Life may rise again
with upright fist—
clasp the sword, and raise it high
against the light—EXCALIBUR!

The new light may burn, an eternal flame —
no shadows — no name.

The Promised Land

There is another place, we're told.
People there do not grow old:
there is no day, there is no night —
just a slow-burning light
to guide you to the Promised Land.

Blue lagoons, cold white sand;
a labyrinth, honey, flowers;
images of singing white choirs;
no time, not even hours;
no moon, no sun, no stars:
just multitudes, snow-white clouds,
Heaven sent.

Humdrum

"It is the humdrum of life," the artist said,
"distorts the picture in my head,
disturbs the poet's gift of rhyme,
scribbles over the author's book:
musicians lose their sense of time."

Timeless culture rides the tide -
will stand on heights sublime -
can itself be born again:
a miracle to hide the shame,
light a torch to stir the flame.

The world does not need humdrum strife.
Restore the quality of life, I pray,
then dawn perhaps will smile on yet another day.

Spring

Winter snows are late this year:
their farewell a dew-drop tear
trembles, then disappears,
has cleansed the ground's green carpet clear:
promises of early spring.
A wild disturbance colour-bound
erupts from pastures, trees and ground —
HARLEQUIN!
But there's no sound as Nature turns herself around,
touches with her magic wand,
and in profusion flowers respond,
deck the earth a velvet hue,
dance and sway a ballet,

as they open the door of life,
Nature's gift to Paradise,
holding the world centre-stage,
and, in poet's book - a page.

Another Spring

Spring - full of hope - a buoyant time
sheds itself from Winter's rime.
Change is in the air:
gently leaves turn to green
after winter, skeletal scene.
Now, full of joy, bud the fronds;
lilies peep from the ponds.
Snowdrops bow their heads:
retire to their summer beds;
giving way to graceful daffodils.
Ballet-like, they dance on hills
and troop the village lanes;
from cuttings curtsy to passing trains.
The world erupts in floral bliss.
Would it always be like this!

River Severn In Spring

The River Severn's in spring-time dress -
has shrugged off winter's flooded stress.
From its upper reaches it tumbles down
via Newtown, Welshpool, Shrewsbury town:
its destination is the sea,
the passing salmon for company.
Cattle now drink at the water's edge;
sand-martins vie for the new-hatched sedge;
otters in mid-stream play:
they feel the water's warmth today.
Old Nog, the heron stands in patient mood,
silent, watchful for frogs and new-spawned food.
At dusk a dash of cinnamon blue -
the flitting kingfisher passes through.

The Confluence of the Severn and Vyrnwy - September 1975

Spring's Wonders

A vibrancy all around: movements disturb the ground.
Winter's tenants having lain, now kiss the sun,
and drink the rain. They erupt across the terrestrial plain,
in a way an artist's brush could never tame.
Creatures travel two by two: swallows herald life anew.
The rasping coot, stepping on lilies in the moat,
answers the field-bound curlew's fluting note.
Carpets of bluebells caress woodland glades,
till evening shadows their beauty shades.
Dawn chorus announces that it's spring.
Perhaps the great Architect's in charge of everything?

Pilgrims' Way

There are pilgrims from across the sea,
seeking their destiny.
They sing a challenging song,
as they slowly walk along.
Their message says, "We do no wrong.
We are here to pronounce
God's gift to man.
Dancing, cymbals fight tears,
destroy stress,
so, 'He who would valiant be,'
come join the path to Calvary,
kneel, pray on bended knee:
heed the message here for thee."

Swaddling Clothes

An image blown across the sky
paints my thoughts, and reasons why we exist.
Creation will not pass us by.
Reproduce – multiply –
Hear the new-born cry.
Rejoice, lift up your heart,
and tread not on the scarecrow's tattered scarf.

The White Steed

God is in his counting-house for things that should not be:
self-destruction, child-abuse, destroying fish at sea;
corruption of the world at large; loss of life at war;
home-grown greed in politics, and many sins more.

God has left his counting-house, lies prostrate on the ground,
praying to forgive our sins,wash away the flaws,
prayers to help your fellow man, become a brimful watering-can
of kindness, joy, others' needs, humility – all those creeds..

Then walk away, if you've found peace:
feel the strength of the strong white steed.
Across his saddle is a sack of promises
made to cleanse the world of bitterness, strife.

Try to lead a better life,
then the wounds from the thorns will heal.
Perhaps some-one somewhere will kneel,
and count our blessings – if they're real.

Beyond Three

Is this the Valley of the Gods?
Is this the Promised Land?
Cool, clear, blue water –
crystal sand.
A soundless music plays,
effortless in every key,
idealistic, moving – odyssey.
Is this the Garden of the Gods?
No darkness – only light.
Great, tall towers
of mystic hue
blend.
Glowing domes,
cascade
well beyond the view –
horizons out of sight.
Anger
does not speak its name –
no burning embers,
no bitter flame.
A tranquil time –
dancing rain
snow-white feathers
tease.
There is a softness, calmness –
no ill-at-ease.
I kiss the ground
where I tread.
"Is this the Valley of the Dead?" I ask.
"No – this is the Promised Land."
He smiled,
and bent to take my hand.

The Blue Lagoon

Tranquil lies the blue lagoon –
softness is its strength –
inviting, kind.
I feel it looks into my mind.
"Do not stray – you are here!
Maybe now, tomorrow, or perhaps another year.
For here there is no Fate, nor Fear,
just a simple step beyond.
The Truth is here to find.
No wounds to heal –
No prayers –
no need to kneel.
The blind will see,
the cripples run,
round the Blue Lagoon:
God's miracle is done.

Graces

May it lift your face,
as touched by the Lord.
Baptise me in the bubbling spring
that has washed away blood from the sword.
I will strive to live the life that I'm given
when released from the umbilical cord.
For in my mother's graciousness
I am her just reward.

May I pass on the joy of life
that has gladdened my heart:
the times of spring,
birds sing,
floral, natural art.
Night fades,

stars wane,
heralding the dawn.
Another day of given time.
I kneel to pray –
making the sign—
thankful to be born.

New Year, Old Year
(2011-12)

Another year has passed us by -
laughter, sorrow - children cry.
Men at war - why must they die
for something so futile?

Then there's drugs -
illicit profit made by thugs.
They abuse the world.
become obscene.

Another year begins anew -
that's the old one gone.
Darkness, shadows, the colour blue -
will the year decide what's true?

Perhaps the missile will pass us by -
"It does not matter," says the clown,
"the circus is back in town:
Parliament sits today!"

Home

Serenity - stands alone -
massive mound of faded brick,
whose chimneys, dramatic, grace the sky.
Picturesque horizon, hugely blessed with loving trees,
their branches bending at their knees,
keep watch, listening to the past
surround this ancient throne,
they are sentinels - they set the tone.

Memories linger - passages of time -
silent, windswept contours survive the scourge of years;
proud, stately porticos have sometime shed tears.
I cannot do it justice, for all the years I roam,
for shadows in the labyrinth have always been my home.

North Front, Loton Park - Mary Parker

Tributes

for Mary Loder *d. 2008*

My garden feels the morning light –
Warmth and comfort from the night.
It has a calmness all its own –
to be there in its stillness.
But you're not alone:
there is poetry in motion -
I sense it in the air –
it's flowers, trees, and birdsong –
they have their village fayre.
Sit still a while and listen
to Nature's orchestral flair,
but remember in my garden
there's always someone there!

for John Hindley
2009 - 90 Not Out

You came to live amongst us -
Coedway your abode.
You are university-trained –
was colourful, we're told.
But the road across the border,
with its ancient, peaceful church
attracted your inner self,
for what you feel is its worth.
Busy - Parish Office -
where I've heard you rock with mirth.
This, John, is where you choose to be:
self-styled 'bishop'- for us, a legacy.

for David Dawson *d. 2010*

Breidden Hill

High on the hill, not far away,
where foxes run
and badgers play,
at twilight fallow deer –
a delight – they softly fade into the night.
Graceful pines in morning mists
sigh gently on the wind.
Buzzards wheel overhead;
ravens from dead carrion feed,
croaking, satisfying their need.
Rain now touches Rodney's throne.
Clouds descend, as in a dome.
The Pillar stands the test of time –
a monument – a worthy shrine.
You have the lordship of the hill:
please walk here, David, at your will.

for Doug Anderson *d. 2010*

You get through the door, among antiques from roof to floor.
cigar smoke lingers in the air: a strong voice rises from a chair.
Hidden by exotic things, enough to make you swoon:
Doug appears - he fills the room.
A man of many interests - quality the theme:
from vintage cars, china dogs - pictures of the Queen.
Cigars - he smoked them every day.
'Fresh from Holland,' he would say. (He gave the odd one away.)
Knowledge of the world he'd gained.
With so much sense he entertained.
I'm glad I went through his door,
but did not end up on the floor.

for John Robjent d. 2012

My Friend

Where did you go, my friend?
I walked the path right to the end.
But there was no sign of you.
Have you gone to join the queue?
This is what souls are meant to do –
or so we are told.

But answer came there none –
only the gulls high in the sky -
their mournful, piercing cries.

What were they trying to tell?
As waves crashed against the shore –
would they tell me more?

I traced my feelings in wet sand.
It read,
"I came to shake your hand.
You know what for.
You'll understand."

for Wolstan Whitaker D.2011

A Shropshire Gentleman

When at last they lay me down,
there is no knocking at my breast.
I will ride my horse up the Shropshire hills,
as the sun dips in the west,
where carpets of snowdrops are nearly past their best –
in contrast, the golden gorse contours a fairy ring.

We pick our way, 'twixt rocks and stones,
where skylarks sometimes sing.
Now at the top I pause a while - my steed will quietly graze.
Down in the hollow, amid the evening haze,
shadows and sunlight compete to stall the ebbing phase,
Music in the valley comes floating up the hill.
It calls me to listen, for hounds are running still.
I hear the call of Wild Edric's horn,
calling them away.
"Do not speak, my beauties, nor make a sound,
for the Master of Winsley has finally gone to ground."

for *Martyn Freeth* *d. 2012*

Waves Of Emotion

The eery cry of the circling gulls
search deep into the soul.
They rise above the crashing surf,
asking questions in their mirth.
Is there birth, is there death?
Does the murmuring, sensual sea
hold mysteries for you and me?
As wandering spirits play
Eternity will have its say.
Did you pass through this way?

for Judy Arliss' lost child

Taken

What shall they do with the souls of the young?
For them, no joy, no songs are sung.
They are not spared, we know not why.
They left the womb:
no blossom,
just tattered flowers, strewn too soon.

for George Mallory and Sandy Irvine

Lost On Everest,

8TH JUNE 1924

Beneath a canopy of white,
horizons stretching out of sight –
picturesque, transparent – needs no candle-light –
just the mists of time:
windswept flanks – a natural shrine.
Guard perished souls where they lie:
there is no need to shed a tear –
endurance beyond fear:
Silent, frozen tombs of ice:
panoramic paradise.